NAVAL WAR COLLEGE
Newport, R.I.

"It's Not the Size of the Dog in the Fight; It's all About Who's Feeding the Dog:

Countering External Support for Insurgency "

Abstract

Nearly all successful insurgencies throughout history have enjoyed some form of external support. Whether it takes the form of political, financial, or military assistance, insurgencies are often dependent upon this support for their survival. It logically follows then that removing that support will severely reduce an insurgency's chances of success. Given the nature of the GWOT, the military planner faces an increasing number of small wars. The first step to winning the hearts and minds is maintaining the security of the population. Disarmament is essential to security.

Table of Contents

Introduction

"The level of activity that we see today from a military standpoint, I think, will clearly decline. I think they're in the last throes, if you will, of the insurgency."- Vice President Cheney to CNN's Larry King, Monday June 20, 2005.

Unfortunately, the Vice President misspoke. As of the writing of this paper, the insurgency in Iraq continues and although the United States is slowly gaining ground, the end is far from near. The question on everyone's mind is how do we win, quickly? The short answer is we don't, but that doesn't mean we can't, eventually. Nearly all successful insurgencies throughout history have enjoyed some form of external support. Whether it takes the form of political, financial, or military assistance, insurgencies are often dependent upon this external support for their survival. It logically follows then that removing this support will severely reduce an insurgency's chances of success.

Background

Insurgencies are not a new development in warfare. The Romans fought countless campaigns against rebellions in Iberia, Gaul, Judea, and Britainnia. Napoleon had his "Spanish Ulcer," and Great Britain faced numerous challenges to colonial rule throughout its empire. While history does provide some examples of successful insurgencies, most have failed. The Romans destroyed Judea. Che Guevara was executed by the government of Bolivia in 1967.[1] The British put down the Mau Mau Revolts of the 1950's. Raul Magsaysay pacified the separatists in the Philippines. The Meo of Laos are nearly extinct.[2] The Sendero Luminoso of Peru is headless. Even the IRA has disarmed.

1

Most insurgencies are doomed from the start. They fail because the government controls the space and has superior force. The application of that force depends upon the political resolve of the state countering the insurgency. The Hungarian revolt of 1958 and the Prague Spring of 1968 are two examples of short-lived and ill-fated insurgencies. Insurgency however, is not always subject to the algebraic equation of forces. If it were so, then a state would only need to maintain overwhelming force to ensure stability. Clausewitz himself stated that, "superiority of numbers in a given engagement is only one of the factors that determine victory. Superior numbers, far from contributing everything, or even a substantial part, to victory, may be actually contributing very little depending on the circumstances." [3]

Superior firepower then is only part of the answer. Are there other means besides firepower available to counter the insurgency? What are the grievances of the insurgents? Can they be addressed? What is the nature of the regime countering the insurgency? What strategy will they employ? What is the geographic nature of the environment? Who is supporting them? These questions illustrate the complexity of counterinsurgency. It would take a significantly larger amount of time and space to answer them, and the solutions would not be universal. This paper addresses the tamer part of the complex problem. What impact does external support have on the operational factors of force, space, and time in an insurgency? Can that support be removed? Will its removal contribute to a successful counterinsurgent strategy? It behooves the operational commander to answer these questions when analyzing an insurgency. Insurgencies vary, but operational factors remain constant. Whichever side is best able to control them will emerge victorious.

Discussion / Analysis

"The presence or absence of external assistance may be the single most important determinant of insurgent war outcome."[4]

As stated earlier, the idea of insurgent warfare is not new to history. Our own nation owes its very existence to the efforts of a foreign funded insurgency. While the British controlled nearly all the major cities and sea ports during the American Revolution, they could not bring the colonists to heel. George Washington knew that as long as the Continental Army existed, the war was not lost. The challenge for Washington lay in keeping that army in the field. At the outset of the war, the Continental Army was untrained and untested. As a result, they could never hope to stand toe to toe with the British regulars dispatched to quell the rebellion. Many of the American soldiers were short term volunteers who came and went with the seasons. When it was time to plant or time to harvest, their ranks would dwindle. Additionally, the lack of uniforms, arms, ammunition, pay, and victories dampened morale and made it difficult for Washington to recruit replacements. Washington relied on time and space to compensate for his lack of force. The British tried repeatedly to engage Washington in pitched battles where they could bring their superior force to bear and destroy his army. Washington continually retreated, declining such decisive engagements in favor of small victories and relying heavily on constant harassment by irregular forces in hopes of undermining his opponent's will to fight. In the end, it was "unconventional militia victories that enabled Washington's conventional army to survive and ultimately triumph. The British lost the war in the countryside."[5] Washington didn't just owe a debt to the militia however. He also enjoyed external support in the form of political, military, and financial aid from the

French. It was their contributions that eventually provided Washington with the force needed to balance his advantages of time and space.

"The American War of Independence turned decisively against the British only after the formation of the Franco-American military alliance of 1778."[6] The French provided enormous amounts of support to the American colonists. Even before the treaty alliance, the government of France provided "$8 million worth of arms, gunpowder, and equipment to the Americans through a dummy trading company, Rodrigue Hortalez & Co."[7] The French military provided troops, ships, and expertise. The French government also provided political assistance by recognizing American independence, extending lines of credit, and applying diplomatic pressure on Great Britain. Perhaps of even greater consequence, France provided indirect external support by threatening Britain's possessions elsewhere in the world and menacing the British home islands. France's intervention enabled the Americans to place the British on the horns of decision. They could sacrifice their holdings in the Caribbean and risk an invasion of their homeland, or they could withdraw from America. Faced with mounting threats abroad and growing political unrest at home, Parliament voted to end the war in 1782. While it is true that many Britons were opposed to the war prior to France's entry, the French intervention gave them a louder voice. "There is probably no more clear-cut example of the importance of outside help to the success of an insurgency than the American War of Independence."[8]

"Unless governments are utterly incompetent, devoid of political will, and lacking in resources, insurgents must normally obtain outside assistance if they are to succeed."[9]

Bard O'Neill should have also added that even when the government is incompetent, foreign assistance is still an insurgent's best chance for victory. Chairman Mao's revolution is one such example, although his support came from an indirect source. In 1925, the Chinese Communist Party was allied with Kuomintang in their struggle against the warlords and imperialists. In 1927, the two factions parted ways and the communists turned to insurgency. By 1934, the Kuomintang had established a central government and Mao's communists were the only challenge to its authority remaining. In order to escape the ever tightening noose of the Kuomintang, Mao led his forces on a 6000 mile retreat, known as the Long March. Nearly 90,000 perished before it was over. Mao willingly sacrificed his force to gain time and space, but his gamble nearly cost him his life. By 1937, Chiang Kai-Shek's Nationalists stood ready to crush the rebellion. Mao had run out of time, space and force. Fortunately for Mao, Japan intervened. The Japanese were not allied with the Chinese communists, and their invasion of China was not timed to provide aid to the beleaguered insurgents; but they saved Mao's revolution. Chiang was forced to break off his pursuit of Mao and face the invaders. While Chiang fought the Japanese in the south, Mao fought them in the north. Their actions against the Japanese invaders provided the communists troops with combat experience and earned them wide spread popular support. "By VJ day, the Party had grown to 1,200,000, controlled an area of 350,000 square miles with a population of 95 million, and had a regular army of 900,000 men and a militia force of 2,400,000. It was no longer vulnerable."[10] The Japanese invasion had given Mao time and some space, but Mao had not won the revolution, yet.

In the final days of World War II, Stalin signed a Treaty of Friendship and Alliance with Chiang Kai-Shek in order to gain access to Manchuria. Stalin doubted Mao's ability to triumph in his revolutionary struggle against the Kuomintang and felt an alliance with the Nationalists would better serve Soviet interests in the Far East. Stalin changed his mind however, once he determined that America was not going to provide troops in support of Chiang's counterinsurgency.[11] Stalin invited the communist Chinese to send political cadres and troops to Soviet held Manchuria. "This permitted Mao to bring the communist revolution to Manchuria and the PLA to contest the KMT's attempt to secure Manchuria for itself upon the departure of Soviet forces. The second benefit was the transfer to the PLA of huge stocks of Japanese arms."[12] Finally, Mao had regained the space and forces necessary to secure victory. Although the material was not the decisive factor in the war--the insurgents in the southern provinces did not have access to it and used captured Kuomintang equipment instead--this windfall enabled the communists to change the nature of the war. While the Japanese equipment may not have impacted the outcome of the war, there is no doubt that it hastened its conclusion.[13]

The success of the Chinese communist revolution demonstrates how external support, even if provided unwittingly, can impact the outcome of the conflict. It also provides evidence on the importance of other types of external support. Apart from force in the form of Japanese military hardware and technical expertise, the Soviets also provided Mao time and space with access to an industrial base gained through international diplomacy and political maneuvering. Clausewitz stated that war is politics by other means. All wars are political; some more than others, and insurgencies more than most.

"The British problem in America was the American problem in Vietnam."[14]

Perhaps more than any other example, the American experience in Vietnam illustrates the importance of external support to an insurgency's success. The agrarian society of North Vietnam could not generate the forces necessary to counter the industrialized might of the United States without some form of outside help. The communist forces in Vietnam relied heavily on the support they received from China and the Soviet Union. There are those who would argue that Vietnam was a civil war fought between the communist north and the corrupt democratic regime in the south. Under this definition, any assistance lent to the Viet Cong by North Vietnam does not qualify as foreign assistance. The only assistance classified as foreign support would be the aid given to the North by China and the Soviet Union. Even so, much of that support in the way of arms, ammunition, and training made its way south to the hands of the Viet Cong. "Indeed, the Communists could not have fought the war or won the way they did without massive support from China and the Soviet Union."[15]

In Vietnam, the factors of time and space also played a significant role. Vietnam is mostly jungle and ill-suited to mechanized warfare. The insurgents controlled the space. Time was also on the insurgent's side. The American people quickly tired of the carnage they saw on the nightly news and their support for the war effort disappeared. Still, regarding the factor of force, the advantage lay squarely on the American side. Or did it? America was a nuclear power, but it is not enough to have superior force unless you're willing to use it. The Soviets and Chinese did not limit their support for North Vietnam to military hardware and expertise. They also provided a much more potent weapon, nuclear deterrence. That nuclear deterrence bridged the force gap between the Army of North Vietnam and the United States.

Much like the French did to the British in the 18th Century, the Chinese placed America on the horns of decision. The United States did not face invasion, but it did face communist challenges elsewhere in the world. The threat of nuclear destruction was ever present and thinly veiled. By the time America involved itself in Vietnam, both the Soviet Union and China had developed nuclear weapons. Arguably, the threat of nuclear holocaust is what kept America from pursuing a more aggressive campaign against the communist insurgents. "In addition to its military and manpower largesse toward North Vietnam, China's very presence north of Hanoi served to limit U.S. military action against North Vietnam."[16] Following the 1968 Tet Offensive, a frustrated General Westmoreland asked President Johnson to escalate the war. "…surely small tactical nuclear weapons would be a way to tell Hanoi something."[17] Johnson however was "determined to avoid any action against North Vietnam that might provoke Chinese intervention."[18] Johnson's advisors shared his concerns and ruled out an invasion of North Vietnam and severely restricted bombing operations near the Chinese border. "They lived with the awesome responsibility of preventing nuclear conflagration and they were thus committed to fighting the war in cold blood."[19] This example illustrates the enormous impact of external support. Not only did the insurgents benefit from foreign military aid, their benefactors were also able to directly influence the strategy of their opponents. "In the final analysis, Chinese deterrence was the main impediment to a more effective…campaign against North Vietnam."[20] External support enabled an insurgency to gain force parity and ultimately emerge victorious.

"If external support is often necessary when insurgents enjoy popular support, it is even more crucial when they do not. Facing a long struggle against government forces with superior arsenals, insurgents must turn to sympathetic nations, other insurgent movements, private institutions in other states, and international organizations."[21]

Hizbollah, Lebanon's Party of God, is an example of an insurgent movement that has grown from a small group of radical terrorists into a major regional political player. Like most successful insurgencies, its support has come from external sources. Lebanon is not an entirely Muslim country. It is a nation comprised of Sunnis, Shiites, Christians, secularists, and Arab nationalists. "Hizbollah emerged out of the context of the Lebanese Civil War (1975-1990) as a splinter-group from the Lebanese Shiite Movement Amal. Amal was founded in the 1960s…to organize Lebanon's deprived Shiite population politically."[22] Lebanese Shiite scholars who had studied under Iranian and Iraqi clerics at the seminary in Najaf, formed the foundation of the movement. They objected to what they saw as the secularization of Amal and felt that Lebanon should fall under Islamic law. "The Iranian revolution in 1979 and the Israeli invasion in 1982 gave further impetus to the fervor of fundamentalist Shiism."[23] The radical clerics found refuge in the Shiite region of southern Lebanon. Hizbollah found space in the mountains of the Bekaa Valley. The central government's preoccupation with Israel and Syria provided Hizbollah with time. Like most insurgencies however, it was lacking force. To gain the force necessary to carry out their revolution, the leaders of Hizbollah turned outward.

Syria resented Israel's incursion into Lebanese territory. Iran was locked in a bloody struggle with Syria's neighbor Iraq. Iran needed Syria to apply pressure to Iraq in the west, and Syria needed Iranian assistance to counter the Israelis in Lebanon.

Hizbollah provided the solution to both countries' problems. In 1982, Tehran and Damascus signed a pact pledging mutual support in their struggles against Iraq and Israel. "During the next years, Iran sent several hundreds of Revolutionary Guards to train Lebanese Shiites in the Bekaa valley under Syrian supervision. The support also extended to military equipment and intelligence."[24] This alliance between a secular Baathist government and Islamist regime provided Hezbollah's founding scholars with access to some of the best equipment and training available. Syria provided an open border to funnel Iranian supplies to the party and augmented its support with limited funds and training camp sites.[25] In addition to the time and space it already enjoyed, Hizbollah now had force, courtesy of external support.

Some would argue that Hizbollah is more an extension of Syrian and Iranian influence than a true insurgency, but that is not the case. Despite its ideological ties to Iranian Shia doctrine, Hizbollah willingly asserts its independence as it continues to grow in strength. Additionally, the movement still professes its dedication to transforming Lebanon into an Islamic republic free from Syrian influence, and they have made great strides in that direction. As of 2006, the Party of God held twelve seats in the Lebanese Parliament (the fourth largest voting bloc) and enjoys the support of most of Lebanon's Shiite population.[26] That popular support is a direct result of their "victory" against Israel in the summer of 2006. That victory, more appropriately termed survival, gained Hizbollah the respect of the Arab world. Of course that victory would have never been possible without the force purchased for Hizbollah courtesy of its allies in Iran and Syria. A Sunni Egyptian interviewed for the International Herald Tribune in 2006 said, "I wish we would send them reinforcements so that they can defend themselves, even if we send them medicine. Hizbollah says that Iran is supporting them. I wish the Arab states would all help Hizbollah too. I am impressed with Iran's role."[27] While Hizbollah's insurgency against the Lebanese government and the Israeli occupation has proven successful, that success could not have come without external support. "The original financial and logistical backing from Iranian sources and NGOs has enabled the Shiites to further integrate into Lebanese society and politics and empowered Hizbollah …to be independent."[28]

The historical examples above prove the vital importance of external support to a successful insurgency and thus support the first part of the thesis. What of the second part? Is the removal of external support an effective counterinsurgency strategy? The answer is yes, but not always. Insurgency is a complex problem and countering external support is only part of the larger solution. Additionally, the operational factor of space will greatly determine the feasibility of removing that support.

"The role of geography, a large one in an ordinary war, may be overriding in a revolutionary war. If the insurgent, with his initial weakness, cannot get any help from geography, he may well be condemned to failure before he starts."[29]

A large, landlocked country with rugged terrain and sympathetic neighbors is ideal for an insurgency. The space is too large for the counterinsurgent to control without massive force. Additionally, external support for the insurgents can flow from any number of quarters. Witness the Soviet problem in Afghanistan. The U.S. was able to use the border with Pakistan to funnel huge amounts of external assistance along with thousands of Arab volunteers through the region to counter the Soviet invasion. "The obvious solution would have been to expand the war into Pakistan."[30] However, expansion of the war was not a politically viable option and would likely prove disastrous militarily. The forbidding nature of the terrain and the international fallout sure to result prevented from expanding the war to Pakistan meant the Soviets were unable to stem the flow of arms or support.[31] The Soviets withdrew from Afghanistan in defeat in 1989.

By contrast, a country isolated by natural borders or bordered by countries opposed to the insurgency favors the counterinsurgent. In the early 1970s, The British and the Sultan of Oman isolated and disarmed the Popular Front for the Liberation of Oman (PFLO), a Marxist movement founded in the 1960s. They were able to do so by effectively interdicting external support for the insurgents. Oman is an isolated, sparsely populated country comprised of mostly desert and mountains. By playing to Arab nationalism, the British were able to counter communist support for the insurgency. "With growing oil revenues, financial aid from other Arab states, and the advent of Iranian troops, the Sultan's Armed Forces, led by British officers, forced the guerrillas back into the arid jabal desert region, confined by an elaborate barbed wire defence line that cut their supply route."[32] Once the flow of arms had stopped, the insurgency was effectively over.

Another example is found in the Malay Emergency of the early 1950's. When communists in the Malay Peninsula rebelled, the British were able to successfully isolate the insurgents and prevented any external assistance from reaching them. Malay is a peninsula and the British were able to control the borders and the maritime approaches. "Over time it was UK/ GOM success in separating the active insurgents from this support which reduced the insurgency to minor proportions."[33]

In some cases, it may not be possible to gain control of the border to remove external support, but compelling a supporter to withhold aid can produce a similar effect. Following World War II, the United States successfully countered a communist insurgency in Greece. The communists were attempting to supplant the pro-western government in Athens and were supported by Tito. The rugged mountainous terrain was uncontrolled, and the insurgents "enjoyed lavish material aid and military guidance from Yugoslavia."[34] By 1947, the communist insurgents controlled nearly eighty percent of the country. However, Tito's support for the insurgency was at odds with Stalin's plans for Western Europe. A purge of insurgent leaders, combined with Stalin's pressure and anti-Yugoslav sentiment amongst the revolutionaries, caused Tito to withdraw his support for the Greek communists. By 1949, the national government had crushed the rebellion and secured Greece's eventual entry into NATO. [35]

Although these examples provide evidence of how removal of external support can contribute to a successful strategy, it is not the sole answer to countering an insurgency. Nor is it always successful. "Remember that the British fought in Cyprus…The Royal Navy sealed off the island from the outside…The ratio between regular troops and guerrillas was 110-to-1 in favor of the British! After five years the British preferred to come to terms with the rebels."[36]

Further proof that countering external support is not universally applicable can be found in French Algiers. "The French very effectively sealed off the Algerian-Tunisian border, and by 1962 had whittled down the guerrillas from 65,000 to 7,000. But the French were winning at the expense of being the second-most-hated country in the world, after South Africa in the UN."[37] Algeria won its independence from France later that same year. The French controlled the space and had an advantage in force, but they did not control the factor of time. Time is arguably the most important factor in an insurgency, particularly when the regime it faces is a democracy.

"Democracies may not have a military center of gravity within an insurgent's reach, but they have a political center of gravity that is vulnerable to indirect pressure: finite public tolerance for a protracted war against an irregular enemy."[38]

Thus far, this paper has focused on the impact of external support as it relates to the operational factor of force. What about the other operational factor of time? Can external support enable an insurgent to gain an advantage in those areas? The operational commander must answer this question when assessing the effectiveness of his counterinsurgency strategy. Given the nature of insurgency, the factor of time is directly related to the nature of the regime. When the counterinsurgent role is played by a democracy, time is generally on the side of the insurgents. There are two reasons for this. First, "democracies fail in small wars because they find it extremely difficult to escalate the level of violence and brutality to that which can secure victory."[39] This is not to say that democracies are above brutality. Countless Japanese and German cities lay in ruins as a result of democratic brutality by the end of World War II. However, World War II was a war fought on a global scale for national survival. An insurgency is a small war. Secondly, a democratic government's mandate only extends to the next election.

General Washington inherently understood this concept and used it to his advantage against the British. By using the spacious interior of the country, Washington was able to avoid capture, buying time for the Revolution. The British public was already divided on the morality of the war. The longer Washington was able to stave off defeat, the more dissatisfied the British became with their government. Additionally, the time bought by Washington's allowed France to marshal it forces, funnel more support to the colonists, and apply ever increasing pressure against the British in other quarters. The Vietnamese also used time to their advantage. The longer the war dragged on, the louder the voices calling for withdrawal. Bui Tin, a former ARVN commander said, "[The U.S. antiwar movement] was essential to our strategy...The American rear was vulnerable. Every day our leadership would listen to the world news over the radio to follow the growth of the American antiwar movement...It gave us confidence in the face of battlefield reverses...America lost the war because of its democracy."[40] As in the case of the American Revolution, the time gained by the insurgents allowed their supporters to provide ever greater amounts of assistance. For the American operational commander facing an insurgency, time is the greater enemy.

Conclusion

The discussion above highlights the critical importance of external support as it relates to operational factors of time, space, and force in an insurgency. When faced with an insurgency, the operational commander must account for external support when developing his courses of action. The feasibility of removing that support is directly dependent upon the space occupied by the insurgency and the time allotted by the regime. Even if it is feasible, the resulting course of action may not be suitable to address the underlying causes of the insurgency. Given the complexities of today's world, controlling a nation's borders may not even be sufficient to interdict external support. The IT explosion and the increased urbanization of the world make counterinsurgency infinitely more challenging. "No longer can a colonial power isolate its colony or client state from the outside world and quietly impose its will."[41]

Recommendations

Perhaps no insurgency better exemplifies this changing dynamic than the current situation in Iraq. Today's insurgent no longer needs a friendly border or sympathetic populace for intelligence and financial support. Continuous media coverage and the internet provide the insurgent with current information and access to external support. Urban sprawl provides the sanctuary previously obtained by remote location. The money flows from countless charitable organizations, legitimate business ventures, numbered accounts, and criminal activities. The landscape of the modern insurgency is increasingly urban and virtual. The lessons learned in the jungles of Vietnam or the deserts of North Africa are not always applicable. "The sophisticated use of modern IT can generate significant support for one's cause through a network of sympathizers and supporters. It is a force multiplier..."[42] History has shown that external support is vital for a successful insurgency. Technology has changed the way that support is obtained. To effectively counter it, this technology must be exploited. Its uses must be given more attention than the passing mention it is afforded in the new Counterinsurgency Manual (FM 3-24).

As populations shift away from rural areas and become more urbanized, identifying and isolating the enemy becomes increasingly difficult. In some cases, it may be impossible to attack the insurgents without incurring prohibitive civilian casualties. This alteration of space means that the commander must seek other battlefields to face the insurgent. By employing more resources in the virtual space, the counterinsurgent can maximize his force in the actual. Just as the presence of external support is vital to the insurgent, its absence is deadly. Remove the support, and the chances of defeating an insurgency increase dramatically. Virtual warfare will not put an end to the grievances that gave rise to the movement any more than conventional warfare would. It will however, contribute to establishing a more secure environment which will permit constructive dialogue. The first goal of any counterinsurgency is to restore security and stop the violence. If we hope to prevail on the ground, we must dominate the ether. Force is on our side. Time is working against us. Space is available. To quote an American poet, "Two out of three ain't bad."[43]

"Clearly the direction in Iraq is headed in a significantly more positive direction than it was five or six months ago." US Defense Secretary Gates, November 1, 2007 responding to question about Iran's pledge to cease arms shipments to the insurgents.

ENDNOTES

[1] Shackley, Theodore. The Third Option. (New York, New York: Dell Publishing, 1981), 69.
[2] Ibid, 3.
[3] Clausewitz, Carl von. On War. Michael Howard and Peter Paret eds. and trans. (Princeton: Princeton University Press, paperback edition, 1989), 204.
[4] Record, Jeffrey. Beating Goliath: Why Insurgencies Win. (Dulles, VA: Potomac Books Incorporated, 2007), 23.
[5] Waghelstein, John D. "Regulars, Irregulars, and Militia: The American Revolution," *Small Wars and Insurgencies* 6, no.2 (Autumn 1995), 136.
[6] Record, 25.
[7] Ibid, 26.
[8] Joes, Anthony James. America and Guerrilla Warfare. (Lexington, KY: University Press of Kentucky, 2000), 47.
[9] O'Neill, Bard. Insurgency and Terrorism: From Revolution to Apocalypse. (Dulles: Potomac Books, Inc., 2005), 139.
[10] Galula, David. Counterinsurgency Warfare: Theory and Practice. (St. Petersburg, FL: Hailer, 2005), 22.
[11] Record, 41.
[12] Ibid 42.
[13] Galula, 26.
[14] Snow, Donald and Dennis Drew. From Lexington to Desert Storm and Beyond: War and Politics in the American Experience, 2nd Ed. (Armonk, NY: M.E. Sharpe, 2000), 32.
[15] Record, 48.
[16] Ibid. 51.
[17] Lewy, Guenter. America in Vietnam. (New York: Oxford University Press, 1978) 128.

[18] Record, 51.

[19] Herring, George C. "In Cold Blood: LBJ's Conduct of Limited War in Vietnam." *The Harmon Memorial Lectures in Military History*. Lecture No.33. (Colorado Springs: U.S. Air Force Academy, 1990), 23.

[20] Lewy, 393.

[21] O'Neill, 139.

[22] Haugbolle, Sune. "The Alliance Between Iran, Syria, and Hizbollah and its Implications for the Political Development in Lebanon and the Middle East." (Copenhagen, Denmark: Danish Institute for International Studies, DIIS Report 2006:10.), 8.

[23] Ibid, 8.

[24] Ibid, 8.

[25] Kramer, Martin. Arab Awakening & Islamic Revival: The Politics of Ideas in the Middle East. (New York: Transaction Publishers, 1996), 212.

[26] Haugbolle, 5.

[27] Slackman, Michael and Mona el-Naggar. "On the Street, Prayers for Hezbollah" (*International Herald Tribune*, July 19, 2006), 2.

[28] Haugbolle, 9.

[29] Galula, 23.

[30] Friedman, Norman. "The Navy, the Cold War-and Now," Proceedings, October 2007 (Vol. 133, pages 58-62), 61.

[31] Record, 53.

[32] Price, D. L. Oman: Insurgency and Development (Conflict Studies, Number 53). (London: The Institute for the Study of Conflict, 1975), 1.

[33] Komer, R.W. "The Malayan Emergency in Retrospect: Organization of a Successful Counterinsurgency Effort." (Santa Monica, CA: RAND, 1972), 9.

[34] O'Ballance, Edgar. The Greek Civil War: 1944-1949. (London: Faber and Faber, 1966), 218.

[35] Ibid.

[36] Fall, Bernard B. 'The Theory and Practice of Insurgency and Counterinsurgency," The Naval War College Review, April 1965 (pages 46-56), 54.

[37] Ibid.

[38] Record, 20.

[39] Merom, Gil. How Democracies Lose Small Wars: State, Society, and the Failures of France in Algeria, Israel in Lebanon, and the United States in Vietnam. (New York: Cambridge University Press, 2003), 15.

[40] Ibid, 22.

[41] Hoffman, Frank G. "Learning Neo-Classical Counterinsurgency," Parameters, Summer 2007 (Vol. 37, No. 2), 73.

[42] Ibid.

[43] Steinman, James. 'Two out of Three Ain;t Bad," (as sung by Meat Loaf on) Bat out of Hell. (Cleveland, OH: Cleveland International Records, 1977), track 7.

BIBLIOGRAPHY

Clausewitz, Carl von. <u>On War</u>. Michael Howard and Peter Paret eds. and trans. Princeton: Princeton University Press, paperback edition, 1989.

Callwell, C.E. <u>Small Wars: Their principles and Practice.</u> 3d ed. Lincoln: University of Nebraska Press, 1996 [1892]

Fall, Bernard B. 'The Theory and Practice of Insurgency and Counterinsurgency," <u>The Naval War College Review</u>, April 1965 (pages 46-56), 54.

Friedman, Norman. "The Navy, the Cold War-and Now," <u>Proceedings</u>, October 2007, Vol. 133, pages 58-62.

Galula, David. <u>Counterinsurgency Warfare: Theory and Practice</u>. St. Petersburg, FL: Hailer, 2005.

Gannon, Kathy. "Hezbollah Fighter's Zeal Undiminished," Yahoo! News, August 22,2006. <u>http://news.yahoo.com</u>.

Haugbolle, Sune. "The Alliance Between Iran, Syria, and Hizbollah and its Implications for the Political Development in Lebanon and the Middle East." Copenhagen, Denmark: Danish Institute for International Studies, DIIS Report 2006:10.

Herring, George C. "In Cold Blood: LBJ's Conduct of Limited War in Vietnam." *The Harmon Memorial Lectures in Military History.* Lecture No.33. Colorado Springs: U.S. Air Force Academy, 1990.

Hoffman, Frank G. "Learning Neo-Classical Counterinsurgency," <u>Parameters</u>, Summer 2007 (Vol. 37, No. 2).

Joes, Anthony James. <u>America and Guerrilla Warfare.</u> Lexington, KY: University Press of Kentucky, 2000.

Komer, R.W. "The Malayan Emergency in Retrospect: Organization of a Successful Counterinsurgency Effort." (Santa Monica, CA: RAND, 1972).

Kramer, Martin. Arab Awakening & Islamic Revival: The Politics of Ideas in the Middle East. New York: Transaction Publishers, 1996.

Lewy, Guenter. America in Vietnam. New York: Oxford University Press, 1978.

Merom, Gil. How democracies Lose Small Wars: State, Society, and the Failures of France in Algeria, Israel in Lebanon, and the United States in Vietnam. New York: Cambridge University Press, 2003.

O'Ballance, Edgar. The Greek Civil War: 1944-1949. (London: Faber and Faber, 1966).

O'Neill, Bard. Insurgency and Terrorism: From Revolution to Apocalypse. Dulles: Potomac Books, Inc., 2005.

Price, D. L. Oman: Insurgency and Development (Conflict Studies, Number 53). London: The Institute for the Study of Conflict, 1975.

Record, Jeffrey. Beating Goliath: Why Insurgencies Win. Dulles, VA: Potomac Books Incorporated, 2007.

Shackley, Theodore. The Third Option. New York, New York: Dell Publishing, 1981.

Slackman, Michael and Mona el-Naggar. "On the Street, Prayers for Hezbollah," International Herald Tribune, July 19, 2006.

Snow, Donald and Dennis Drew. From Lexington to Desert Storm and Beyond: War and Politics in the American Experience, 2nd Ed. Armonk, NY: M.E. Sharpe, 2000,32.

Steinman, James. "Two out of Three Ain't Bad," (as sung by Meat Loaf on) Bat out of Hell. (Cleveland, OH: Cleveland International Records, 1977).

Sun Tzu. <u>The Art of War.</u> Samuel B. Griffith, trans. Oxford: Oxford University Press, 1980.

Waghelstein, John D. "Regulars, Irregulars, and Militia: The American Revolution," *Small Wars and Insurgencies* 6, no.2 (Autumn 1995)